2

T0372119

Amelia Earhart

Caroline Crosson Gilpin

Washington, D.C.

Published by Collins
An imprint of HarperCollins *Publishers*
The News Building, 1 London Bridge Street,
London SE1 9GF
HarperCollins Publishers
Macken House, 39/40 Mayor Street Upper,
Dublin 1, DO1 C9W8, Ireland

Browse the complete Collins catalogue at
www.collins.co.uk

In association with National Geographic Partners, LLC

NATIONAL GEOGRAPHIC and the Yellow Border Design
are trademarks of the National Geographic Society,
used under license.

Second edition 2018
First published 2013

ISBN 978-0-00-831716-4

10 9 8 7 6 5

A catalogue record for this book is available from the
British Library

Printed by Pureprint, UK

If you would like to comment on any aspect of this
book, please contact us at the above address or
online.
natgeokidsbooks.co.uk
cseducation@harpercollins.co.uk

Paper from responsible sources

Since 1888, the National Geographic Society has
funded more than 12,000 research, exploration, and
preservation projects around the world. The Society
receives funds from National Geographic Partners,
LLC, funded in part by your purchase. A portion of the
proceeds from this book supports this vital work. To
learn more, visit http://natgeo.com/info.

Photo Credits

Table of Contents

Who was Amelia Earhart?

Aeroplanes were new in the 1920s.
People mostly travelled by car or
boat or train. But Amelia Earhart
dreamed of flying.

Amelia was one of the first women
pilots. She was known all over the
world. She did many things women
had never done before.

Growing Up

The house where Amelia was born

Amelia Mary Earhart was born on July 24, 1897.

She grew up in the state of Kansas in the USA.

She loved playing with her sister, Muriel. Together they played sports, went fishing and collected insects. They also enjoyed reading.

Back then girls wore long dresses. But Amelia's mother made them playsuits. Then they could run and play like the boys.

In Her Own Words

"I believe that women have as much courage as men."

Amelia's family moved a lot. She went to many different schools. Luckily, Amelia made friends easily, and she enjoyed making people laugh.

When Amelia grew up, she worked as a nurse. Later, she worked at a centre that helped poor children. The children loved her.

Amelia loved to help people.

Amelia in her nurse's uniform

A Love of Flying

When Amelia was 23, her father took her to an air show. She took a short ride in an aeroplane that day, and she fell in love with flying.

In Her Own Words

"As soon as we left the ground, I knew I myself had to fly."

Amelia with the first plane she owned

Amelia wanted to be a pilot.
She worked hard to earn money
for lessons.

Amelia's first teacher was pilot Neta Snook.

In Her Time

Many things were different in the late 1920s and 1930s.

Jobs

Most people did not have a lot of money. There were not many jobs.

Cars

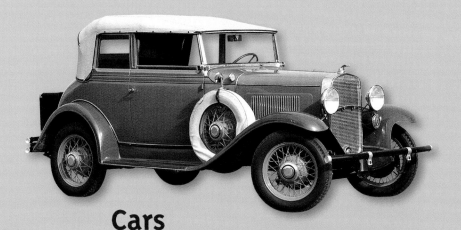

Cars were much slower than they are today. They couldn't go very far, either.

Fun

People played board games for fun.

Radio

People did not have TVs in their homes. Most people listened to the radio.

Women

Finding jobs was harder for women than for men. Some people thought women shouldn't work outside the home.

Amelia always tried to do better. She flew fast. She flew high.

Amelia wanted to be the first woman pilot to cross the Atlantic Ocean. It was very dangerous. Many people had died trying.

But in 1932, she made the long, hard trip, and she did it – all by herself.

In Her Own Words

"Adventure is worthwhile in itself."

Becoming Famous

Amelia Earhart was becoming famous. She was well known because she was a great pilot, but also because she was a female pilot.

In Her Own Words

"Women must try to do things as men have tried."

Amelia taught female college students about jobs and careers.

Not many women had careers in the 1930s. But Amelia did. She showed other women they could have careers, too.

Words to Know

CAREER: A person's life work

Amelia wrote books about her flying career. She gave speeches all over the USA. In 1933, she was invited to the White House, where the American President, Franklin Roosevelt, lived.

Amelia became friends with the President's wife, Eleanor Roosevelt. She took Mrs Roosevelt for a ride in her plane. Mrs Roosevelt wished she could be a pilot, too.

The White House

Amelia and Eleanor Roosevelt agreed that women could do the same kinds of jobs as men.

Amelia the Hero

Amelia got many awards and medals. She spoke to college students about aviation.

People everywhere wanted to be like her.

Words to Know

AVIATION: The world of flying and aeroplanes

Amelia at Purdue University in the USA.

Amelia was not afraid to try new things, and she never gave up. She was a hero for many people.

Amelia helped test a parachute.

Amelia was the first woman to get this medal. It is the US Distinguished Flying Cross.

6 Fun Facts About Amelia

1

Amelia drank hot cocoa and ate oranges on her plane trips.

2

Pilots used to be called "aviators". The word comes from "avis", which means "bird" in Latin.

3

Amelia married George Putnam in 1931. He published books. He helped Amelia with her career.

4

One of Amelia's planes is at the Smithsonian National Air and Space Museum. It's in Washington, D.C. in the USA.

5

Amelia was the first president of the Ninety-Nines. This is a group of women flyers.

6

Amelia had her own US postage stamp! It came out in 1963.

Around the Globe

Amelia always dreamed of flying around the world. She got a bigger, faster plane to make the trip.

Amelia took Fred Noonan with her. He was her navigator.

His job was to give directions. Amelia's job was to fly the plane.

Words to Know

NAVIGATOR: A person who uses maps to help find the way

In Her Own Words

"Flying may not be all plain sailing, but the fun of it is worth the price."

The Last Flight

Amelia and Fred flew for one month. They flew across deserts and mountains.

But the hard part was next. They had to fly over the huge Pacific Ocean.

A Lockheed Electra 10E aeroplane, the same model Amelia used in her flight around the world

1897
Born July 24 in
Atchison, Kansas, USA

1916
Graduates from
high school

1918
Works as a Red
Cross nurse

The cockpit of Amelia's plane

They needed to stop for fuel on a tiny island that was hard to find in the large Pacific Ocean. On July 2, 1937, Amelia and Fred took off from their final stop and headed for the island.

1921
Learns to fly from pilot Neta Snook. Buys her first aeroplane.

1922
Sets record for highest flying, at 14,000 feet (4,267 metres)

1926
Works at a children's centre in Boston, USA

Suddenly, the plane couldn't be reached by radio. No one is sure what happened. Many people believe the plane ran out of fuel and crashed. Amelia and Fred were never found.

Amelia Earhart was a great pilot. She taught others to live without fear. She was loved by people all over the world.

1930
Sets record for fastest flying, at 181 miles an hour

1931
Marries book publisher George Putnam

1932
Flies across the Atlantic Ocean alone, landing in Ireland

Amelia's final flight

where Amelia flew
stops she made
not all stops are shown

ASIA

EUROPE

NORTH
AMERICA

start

West
Africa

AFRICA

Pakistan

California

Florida

Ethiopia

Thailand

New
Guinea

Amelia disappears
over the Pacific Ocean

AUSTRALIA

Brazil

SOUTH
AMERICA

1936

Purdue University gives
Amelia money to buy
a Lockheed Electra 10E
aeroplane

1937

Sets off to fly
around the world.
Disappears
July 2, 1937.

2012

New search begins
for Amelia's plane.
Nothing concrete
found yet.

What in the World?

These pictures show close-up views of items from Amelia Earhart's time. Use the hints to work out what's in the pictures. Answers are on page 31.

HINT: A machine used to fly

HINT: It protects your head.

HINT: They cover your eyes.

HINT: An award

HINT: You can use this to find your way.

HINT: It goes on a letter.

Answers: 1. aeroplane, 2. helmet, 3. goggles, 4. medal, 5. map, 6. stamp

Glossary

AVIATION: The world of flying and aeroplanes

CAREER: A person's life work

NAVIGATOR: A person who uses maps to help find the way

PILOT: A person who flies an aeroplane